Bee Dance

Bee Dance

Cathy Cain

A Publication of The Poetry Box®

Editing & Book Design by Shawn Aveningo Sanders
Cover Illustration & Design by Robert R. Sanders
Author photo by Alex Cain

ISBN: 978-1-948461-22-1
Library of Congress Control Number: 2019938586

Printed in the United States of America.

Published by The Poetry Box®, 2019
Beaverton, Oregon
ThePoetryBox.com

With love to my family and dear friends ...

—*Where we gather meaning and pleasure in our lives, the energy and gesture of that dance, these are things I think about.*

– Contents –

Histories of Home

Riding the Disturbance

Pink Mist of Morning

Hint of Blue Promise

Holding Rock

Hint of Hexagon

Please give me a safer read
beyond the headlines   one I can handle
like the story about the cloud cover
around Saturn's north pole
how it gathers and swirls in a handsome hexagon
a fearsome harmony

The shape of that cloud
like the center scutes on an ancient tortoise shell
or the veined delineation of a cicada wing
or carbon that sits in graphite   nests in diamonds
like columnar basalt cooling
like each snowflake's crystal clinging

Space ordered to protect its content of beauty
There are fairy rings in Africa and Australia
harsh climates where plants cooperate for water
and settle along six-sided perimeters
of emptiness   a pattern that makes room
amid Nature's indifference   for a content of beauty

The bee's honeycomb
a clean design
so unlike our amorphous perversity
This family of man falling   lost
The buzzing hum of alarm
among our torn wax tatters of grace

But then today's science news
Our remembered paths to place
our own nerve tracts
may also be loosely packed

[. . .]

as if in a beehive
a hint of hexagon

The pleasure of pattern
a map
through the rough human expanse
between perfect flower and honey trance
I could show you where I've been
do my best bee dance

California Buzz

I miss the hum
of golden pollinators, thick
honeybee in yellow acacia.
Blossom fuzz dusting

the tree swing's mellow trance,
the Dutch door to the playhouse.
Honeysuckle sunned out
against a white fence.

Beyond, the small plot
of orange and lemon trees.
Hours, heavy with scent,
low enough to pluck.

Even, under that rock,
the black widow hanging,
red hourglass warning.
You could skirt her with luck.

Dawn Fire

A large eucalyptus branch burst
into flowered flame, crashed downward.
The hillside across the bay blazed
with bright orange, sharp-edged dartings.

Clamoring, insistent sizzle.
Riddled birds arced, flew far.
Wind fanned fire's amoral reach
of wordless thirst, dazzling argument.

                                                  ❧

But I did not want to follow
that line of reasoning.
I yearned for a different light,
one I could absorb, become,

a quiet light so satisfying, soon
I would vanish, moon-like, behind
the flashing fire of daybreak's burning.
I turned my gaze to the bay.

There, a small white ship pasted on a pale blue sea.
Above, not yet rouged by smoky haze,
hung the full white moon, faint and fine,
complete within its soundless solitude.

A white ship fading into pale sea.
The white moon, there, on the white blue sky,
reflecting back all color
into the dark acceptance of my empty eye.

Josephine and Rose

Voices of the film crew
parked at Josephine and Rose
rise above their white tech vans
as fog lifts the Berkeley hills.

Bungalows with their baskets
of broken hearts hunker down
amid pungent pine, eucalyptus,
bougainvillea and trumpet vine.

Skirting ice plant, a woman
in her yellow-fringed shawl
walks below the mural
painted with an eagle and a rose.

In nearby windows, protected
from the wind, faces try intensely
to hold their own against
a city's expectations.

There are blue forget-me-nots
at the edge of the bay
where redwing blackbirds
careen with impulse.

Caught on film, the distant bridge span
shines, stays memory.

Rock

passing cars   truck brakes   sirens
city sounds from below
filter up through the window
of the Victorian apartment as I write
with only myself for talk

my words are so simple
perhaps also my thoughts
yet I return to them
for the same comfort
I receive from holding rock

The Lady from Texas

She'd always had a hankering for
a tumbleweed, nimbly rambling its bouncy
bottom across the state of Texas.

The acres of windswept landscape
she owned and jealously guarded
spoke of her fierce longing for wilderness
that kept her apart, alone.

If she could corral just one
rootless singularity, bring it home,
untangled from the wind,
she could break it in, have a friend.

&

She would center the tumbleweed
in an empty, large-windowed room.
There it would settle, finely wrought, calmed, content
with space enough, protected from driving gusts.

&

She finally snared one, afield, in a dry gulch,
rough, like a stray dog begging the driver at a truck stop
for pity, for food, for water.
She took it home,

but soon discovered that the thorny
roving tumbleweed fought being contained.
Its tiny barbs freed themselves, untamed,
dropped on the bare oak floor, nagged at her peace.

[...]

She knew rest would only come when
she released her prize back to the wild
undefined and airy truth
flowing through our fretwork frames.

⁓

Sitting alone at the black iron table
under the pepper tree's sparse shade
with a few potted cacti and bougainvilleas,
she took a sip of whiskey and sighed surrender.

Let the wind, instead, declare her yearning,
bounce it high out there.
Free it in wide open lands.
A dream rolling, rolling.

Sonoran Tapestry

I walk this desert like
a needle poised above velvet

Here, white bursage
mounds the fragrance of morning light

My breath a thread   a silken whisper
Each step a stitch of space

Saguaro   barrel   pincushion
prickly pear   and ocotillo   My bones

glide   lizard rustle   creosote sigh
glowing cholla cactus spine

Buried mountain shoulders
channel an occasional flash flood

an anecdotal alluvial fan
Great seas advance   recede

Open   quiet   embroidered land
rich with bones   with bones

No Matter What the Name

In a hidden dimension, a force held back
through eons, waited for
that first pink bud to coalesce,
waited for us, the fleshy namers.

Now, in the quiet of the night,
we gaze at the stars
and into the depths between each star.
We hunger to name what we sense—
circle, symmetry, honesty,
an elusive elegant proof.

We crave the gravity of poetry to help us
bend the light of our particular experience
and give title to our peculiar paradox.
Sometimes, we come close.

Deeper into
the Forest Thicket

Trail Guide

A sign nestles in the forest.
Look for the trailhead.
Moderate up hill.
At first, the hiker is faced with open country.

Along both banks of the creek, wildflowers
on thin stalks appear barely there,
but they are bountiful in season.
Please leave them for others to enjoy.

The falls are upstream.
They can be reached by paralleling
the brook or the lifeline
on the palm of your hand.

Be prepared for spots of mud
and sweet, needled pine.
One fallen cone. Many.
Mottles of sunshine.

Hazard alert: Rattlesnakes are common.
Circumnavigate.
Near the rim top, the trail is ill-defined.
Proceed to the precipice.

It is not a loop trail.
Always let someone know
where you are hiking and
if you plan to return.

[. . .]

You will see a series of small lakes,
all blue. You can swim in their skies.
The trail passes by Paradise.
You may catch a glimpse.

Waiting for Chance

chance   like a tree discovered
    chance   not a narrative already told
the world so thinly sliced   catching
      every body off   balance
precarious potential
       a shift of weight

your knee bends   your hand reaches out
    you lean in
to smell gnarled bark
    this   your chance

Quotidian Purls

first a single chirp
then another
like the stars
who come to visit
one by one
until we register
galaxy   universe

the sun's vertical white stripe
along one tree trunk's eastern edge
strikes out clean
against adjacent bark's deeper gray
then repeats to form
an irregular pattern
among the long grasses
until we realize
aspen   grove

and the green fire
of morning grass
first illumined
birthed from night's dark womb
complements our faces
shows them more rosy against the green
until we cry out
life

first a single chirp
then another

Damp

Among licorice fern, the gurgle
of hidden streams, and the detritus of decay,
live the spirit mothers of the Sitka forest.
With sudden quick rustles, they glide
from bough to bough   whisper to each other.

Deep in the shadows,
these sisters of the green
mine veins of dappled light
from the dark and mossy histories
of forgotten love   love irrepressible.

And now, the eldest few, damp and aged,
almost invisible, like mist, gather once again
to hold hands at the fringe of trees around
a clearing of open sunshine.

Here, near the pungent clumps of yellow skunk cabbage,
they teach one younger sister
about unblinding birth,
how it is marked by a bright, sharp edge.

Pushing

a quickened doe
gliding deeper
into forest thicket

nostrils flared panting
gold rock eye
warm centered alert

through sparkling rush of birth
private my power
secret my creation

Shy

The bent and shrunken woman
standing under an aged alder
whose mossy branches
mimic her long white hair

Standing under an aged alder
her dry blind bones
hidden beneath her long white hair
she calls the deer

With dry blind bones
and hand held out
she calls the deer
offers food in silence

Her hand held out   the deer nears
A shy gesture by each
giving and receiving in silence
life to life

A shy gesture by each
under those mossy branches
Life to life
Deer with bent woman rising

Sitting Cross-Legged in the Forest, I Become *Peziza*, an Upturned Cup Mushroom

My hands form a cup of spores, each an ornamented dream.
Come now, rain, with your clear and focused drops,
splash my spores far into this forest gleam.

Come now, breeze, touch my smooth curve,
blow loose my tightly-wrought, unwinding themes,
disperse them through this woodland's woven texture.

My secret source of growth
has prospered, like that in violet fairy, scarlet cup, and mature
rindy orange peel, enclosed

and hidden in hyphae sprung from mycelium root.
Through the many years, I have composed
a fertile arc within this ripened fruit.

In my lap, one hand holds, cups, the other.
My silence bursts, no longer mute,
a hymenium remnant, a pregnant mother,

receptive bowl, full of me and not me.
Spore by spore, reveries rise together,
expose an ecology of elaborate story.

I remain ready to greet the rain.
Listen for the longing of letters, hungry
to reveal my name.

Small Blessings

To the forked tree crook:
Thank you for the view through.

To red elderberry:
You've soothed the nettle's sting.

Birdcall:
I hear you.

Tip of bird's beak:
Sure, point the way.

New sword fern frond:
Help me uncurl.

To candy flower's pink cloud floating above nurse log:
Dissolve me.

To woodpile's inky, hidden chinks:
Bless your secret darks.

One for each of us,
so we know we're not alone.

Weather Gathering

Drumbeat and downpour.

The thundering dragon gathers his fiery lightning

and dark weight,

ambles off in the mist.

I go with him.

I ride his silver spoon scales

under parting clouds.

By moonlight we gather

the quiet of water.

We leave a trail that meanders

like drips down

a tall arched window pane,

like sweat from barefoot dancing

that pools in small shining puddles

on a pale wood floor.

Courtship

Enticing him
with her veil
of Spanish moss,
the yew sustains,

prolongs
a tender kiss
from that huge boulder
leaning down on her.

While he inclines,
she designs
their courting
through the years.

Provocative, she knows
her root's strong hold,
the slow wisdom
of swollen sensation.

Histories of Home

Columbia River Basalt

ponder the uneven flow of viscous liquid
through geological time
hot material upwelling
strata differentiated by temperature   and density
earth's mantel permitting magma convection
a slow thick chaotic process

ponder sudden eruptions from fissures
a lava flood stretching
tens of miles per day   from Idaho to sea
inter-fingering   of soft sediments and sand
small explosions spewing along the way
while ponding to depths half a mile or more

ponder this blooming plume communing
with the base of our neighborhood
streets   trees   schools   houses   us

Fallen

I am not the mole who senses
each light human step
as an abrupt elevator drop reverberating
through tender, damp and wormy soil.

It took the flop of a century-old Douglas fir
a block away to thud my stomach,
make it lurch, as the ground under me jolted,
then shook in splendid recovery.

Massive downrush, soft green bough,
ring-marked seasons, layered
smell of sticky, sweet sap,
nests with their histories of home.

Did those small men even register what they'd done?
The cataract force,
the slow-motion keel,
enough to make a grown woman cry.

An eagle banked, hovered low under azure sky,
circled wide with deliberate measure, five times
around, then soared. The animals know.
They witness for the mighty, now laid prone.

Screen Saver

This coursing electricity gives, perhaps,
an insight into the space of synapse
charged with the swift current of mind.

Binary—no imbalance exists.
One or zero, on or off,
heartbeat of our virtual life.

How ironic that a manmade machine
becomes the new vehicle
beckoning us through light to the immaterial.

I flow into the screen-saver photo
of my husband's young face, so ethereal.
Light bounces back even from

the folds of his hair, black
like the night of thought
wording history, fiction, or poem,

dense as a night birthing stars,
heavy suns that pull us toward their blinding,
burn away our questions.

While others sleep, I write.
The slow black font of my conceit
grows incandescent, white with heat.

I sit naked alone in the thick summer night,
my skin glowing with a blue halo
of cool sleepless light.

Hunger

The bright path of green curiosity
hangs ripe with fruit
on your screen's shifting display.
Light's weight entices,
and you reach for an image
as you step into this wondrous way.

You enter a binary garden,
a lush quartz maze,
open tiny etched latches
on simple, red, logic gates.
What of this abundance have you yet to taste?
Will it nourish, or offend?

With gravitas, you take another byte,
eat this garden's lovely light.

Lichen from Heaven, Threatened

Rock tripe, witch's hair, British soldiers,
old man's beard, pixie cup, map, and *lecanora*.

Some in the Arctic were blown across mountain sweeps
    and vast deserts,
some held dyes for Scottish tweeds,
some held hope for lepers.

Some held thirty times their weight in water,
life for caribou, color for the tundra.

Some held time, eight thousand years, as if
in suspended animation, for ancient Greenlanders,
but maybe not for us.

Lifeline

I once saw a diagram in a book
showing a segment of Earth's curve
the small band of biosphere
belying its abundance of life
Beyond that   the depth of our atmosphere
displayed as a mere line
pencil-point thin   a fine film
like your lover's skin

skin you desire   skin you smell

You breathe in familiar delight
yet often wish its accompanying care
would disappear
relief if the burden were not there

Now   seeps in
the wrong kind of heat
a lack of fresh air
small extinctions underfoot

You touch Earth
take your pleasure
but compromise her
with hurt   like a knife
bruise open her skin
deny   how it protects her life

pencil-point thin
a fragile line

I once saw a diagram in a book

Burn

Blue eucalyptus and the acrid ooze
of black oil under water's shine
Wooly mammoths and saber tooth tigers
trapped ages ago in the La Brea tar pits

And now this plastic made to look like water
like stainless steel   wooden floors   like leather
wine corks   flowers   an eyelash   or a breast

Man's toxic brilliance reeks
as the sunny sky heats up
Humans caught mid-gesture   sinking beneath
the sparkle of our machine-made objects

The quickly rising sludge
of plastic's slow burn
an arm reaching out

Dust on Water

We are dust on water.
We skate on a granite meringue,
an old primordial melt with exquisite surface tension
fractured now, not only by God.

River reflections, like ancient boatmen,
flash signals to us—mica light, schist and sheen,
silica and cellulose.

Blue chicory, periwinkle thistle,
and Queen Anne's lace on the banks above
could light our journey, but we're lost.

We've forgotten, like threatened salmon,
our loamy way through layers of thirst—
no genetic imprint left to encourage our return—
a handful thrown wide to the wind.

Riding the Disturbance

The News Hour 2009

Why has no one

mentioned
      that aching beauty

                       the silent sky
above the ravaged desert of Iraq

      indigo blue

studded
      with eons of watery stars?

Tsunami

Great heaves of dark energy hurl galaxies
clouds of light   like pale gray whales flung far
rolling   spiraling   through the vast salty silence

Each vortex wraps its roiled curl around
and warps waves of midnight-blue

Torn from each other   among the velvet folds
the galaxies sing long high-pitched sounds
mournful travelers   riding the disturbance alone

Without Defense

Their swim suits mimic the surf's crisp blue sheen,
bare skin echoes wet sand, dark and rich.
Two young brothers, maybe twelve and fourteen.
One waits, one skims. Then they switch in morning mist,

arms and hands extended, poised. Grace
in perfect balance. Most moments, youth slides
sideways with ease, like these playful boys'
wager against cold waves and boiling sea.

They laugh when sludge, grey rock, or deep water
brings each up short, crashing without defense.
When will the sure surge roar in
to undo their cool, upright innocence?

For now, engaging the sea with a glinting glide,
they throw the board, thinking only of the ride.

Terra Preta Nova
(New Dark Earth)

Lay me with the ash of my evening fires,
the warm white shards of my bowls and mugs,
my leavings of tomato, cilantro, cinnamon,
and heavy wholesome bread.

Place me with the charcoal remains
of my paintings, letters, and books.

My body will soften into rich humus,
into that dark smell that speaks
of damp jungles, forests untouched.

I will join the life force of new black earth,
your terra preta nova, for millennia or more.
I will remediate your future.

Nectar

When the flower dies,
how long does its nectar remain?
How could this gold pollen not sweeten the earth?

Who will dig our bones long after?
Will we be cased in museums of amber
or in rich black tar?

Will our remains be read
with proper attention
to our courage and gentle ways?

Will our white bones reveal
the soft flesh and lush juice of our lives,
the light that now glows in your eyes?

Aquanaut

She runs the water
rinses her teeth before bed
balances on one foot
and confronts the mirror
Where did we come from?
Bamboozled   she spits thanks anyway
for toast and tomorrows
toothpaste too
She stands on the other foot
asks the mirror
You mean   I am   then not?

She travels into the mirror
light years   fathoms
the diving bell of her   like a little bug
a constellation   or our galaxy
with its ancient offering of stars and space
She brushes the Milky Way of her hair
throws off shooting stars
searchlights through the depths of night's water

Pink Mist of Morning

Dream of a List of Names

I will live in the forest with the fairies
and carry a wishbone   split like my legs
open to night's home   home of dreams
pomegranate dreams   ruby seed dreams

I have in my heart the list of our names
mine   yours
that were caught in our ruthless digital life
in tangled data nets of numbered identities

I hacked the machines
deleted our names   left holes instead
slashed the cold screen   into a leafy fretwork
wounds of excision   the price of freedom

Now among the trees I drip an inky trail
With my feather quill I rewrite our names by hand
pull them back
through the holes   birth them

once more into flesh
I wish us back here
loosened
blood seeds glistening

to walk singing   into our dreams
damp earth   scented fir
The forest canopy sways
bursts with the flight of birds

Bottari, a Wrapping Cloth

It's so exhausting not to trust the universe,
to carry the earth hidden in my midnight-blue *bottari*,
that weighty bundle I have hauled
for so long on my slightly-bent back.

Now old enough to wonder,
Was I able to protect anything?
I finally let go—drop my shoulder,
lower the knotted corners I have held with cramped hands,
then slide this importance off my back,
lay it gently down.
I exhale, untie the four corners,
and let the cloth fall open, flatten with the slack.

At first they freeze—
the miniature elk, the deer, and the squirrel—
startled by the light. They sniff the air.
Then one blinks an eye.
Slowly, the elk turns her head, focuses her gaze farther out.
The fern, salal, and Douglas fir,
the pine, and redwoods I have carried
release themselves from each other.
The sequoia unseals its stomata.

One by one the animals—
elk, deer, squirrel, skunk, slug, and wolf —
slowly glide over the edge of the cool, silk square.
Two chickadee fly.
I listen to my eased breath.
Each animal enlarges as it moves out
into the pink mist of morning.

House of Rain

rain night rain
rain of dreams
my little boat careening

through watery nightmare
drench of navigating
the curtained interior roar

finally the reign of morning
rain my body rain
a calm rocking in dawn's civil twilight

at last a trust in water
rain glinting rain
as I row towards open day

through this shining scrim
lit waterfall of my skin

Cold Pizza for Breakfast

She rises and walks barefoot down the sunny road
through the grey-shingled village still sleeping,
out to the fresh-laid sand and sapphire sea.

All perfect, meant to be.
She unwraps a briny breakfast,
savory slices of a salty scene—

bright tomato starfish, Kalamata olive snails,
onion urchins and garlic clove bivalves,
aubergine mussels with their soft inner clinging.

Water waves in cheesy, mushroomy, roiled-sand muck,
and red pepper kelp. Not too sweet,
just as she wishes the coming day.

She approaches the ocean's cold shock,
her hand touching rough, barnacled rock.

Whelk

I used to dread the drive
through the long curved roar
of the Vista Ridge Tunnel,
walled with glossy, cream-colored tile.
But I've learned that brake lights swoosh it
pearly pink, make an iridescent interior,
a whorl, a whelk, a cochlea.

And if I swirl my liquid spirit
as I curl through this tunnel,
I become the hum,
the sum of open sea,
expanded, savored
the way a shell holds the shape
of the farthest sound.

The Man from Wind Thin

He was high enough in the fir tree
that I had to crook my neck to see him.
He dug in his boot spurs, leaned back, stiff,
straight from the tether of his yellow lanyard.
The acute angle of empty space
that his body made with the trunk.
The chainsaw dangling from
a second rope attached to his waist.

How I sensed his breath as he pulled up the rope,
set saw to tree.
The sudden roar.
The spew of pale chips caught
in afternoon light like the tail of a comet,
like a cloud of fireworks.
The weight of visual drop.
The thud.
The spot of nothing above.
How we hold on to nothing
before the blue sky fills in.

The Finishers

When I write, I talk to myself
as if there are two of me.
We work side by side,
creature and consciousness,
often we bump elbows.

&

I drive through the freeway construction
early mornings after I write.
There, I follow two men
held high in a cherry-picker,
their silhouettes small
against a massive new concrete wall.

They inch along
sanding off the delicate line,
the overlap, of yesterday's wet work.

&

Between us, we move mere mud
and more, move memory,
move a concrete image,
like a pond at dawn
in a field near an old barn.
Throughout the heated day,
the pond's boundary where pure water
touches mud, makes the mere idea
of wall, of boundary a slippery absolute.
We make much of the smallest mere.

[…]

⌒

Two quiet men standing in a basket,
each in a sun-yellow hard hat,
erasing yesterday's potency
for the birth of today,
their shoulders often touching.

⌒

We tangle small sticks in cross-outs,
confront rough spots, aim to smooth
a seamless structure
to hold our astonishments
as if we could ever finish this fashioning.

Kiteboarder at Road's End

Sunshine reflects off his black wetsuit back to God
before the wind releases him into the hovering fog.
He sails heartily at breakneck speed
before he's lost in the gray water or cloud.

As I watch, I have only a pocket notebook
and found words to tack, hold back
the water that takes us all down
unless we skim with the wind, color sailing free.

Harnessed in, yet handling well the icy thrill,
the sudden jerk, dip, and douse. The lift,
then the tack, that rakish angle,
as my hand reaches down to touch the water.

My Middle Name

Eventually, I will become less me,
more amorphous and fuzzy in structure,
more uniform in appearance, until
a point of stability
is achieved,
a limit of decay.

Difficult to define
in precise terms,
I will remain
a highly complex substance,
the complete nature of which
we do not fully understand.

But know: I will remain.
Carbon is my middle name.

Hint of Blue Promise

Yes

Day's warm unwinding empties,
ends as a flattened cloth, a blue darkness,
a raven's wing.

Stars and galaxies, even Andromeda,
a beauty 220,000 light-years wide,
begin to whisper their wild orchestrations.

The Oldest Metaphor

effusive foam blows free
a rich white litter across the littoral zone
mother earth is replete   overcome
small schooner clouds skim across
her moist sandy shore

among afternoon's white silvers
waves still surge after the storm
earth   spent   glistens
misty possibility
widened by the wind
her wet womb mirrors the sky
with a hint of blue promise

Flex

this cloud like a rock
like an airborne boat
come to carry me away
sunny slant-lit rain pours over me
I spread my arms palms up
from the tips of my fingers
silver shimmers down

with deepening breath
I throw back my head
open my mouth
and drink the water
inhale the light
flex my thighs
leap aboard

Cozy

smooth grey beach rocks
take shelter
on my closet floor

hunker in my car trunk
sleep down under my bed
hide out in my basement boxes
and nestle in my lingerie drawer

they cozy my body
quiet my mind
lighten my heart

Platonic

His Words:
Hag of my heart, the shag of your bark,
a century old, droops off. I have stood
at a distance this long time, too far apart for touch.
But through the windowed openings
between my mullioned branches, I have watched you.
My solid, upright, furrowed skin, single.
You in your niche, I in mine.

Hers:
We have kept our distance.
Yet under spring's green oxalis, bleeding heart,
and each autumn's leaf fall,
beneath the surface of rich and mossy detritus,
at the end, as we lean toward each other, or away,
we will find that our roots, through our long affection,
have, indeed, mingled simply and discreetly.

On the Malvern Hills, England

We've had a setback the last few years
due to who knows what   virus
pestilence   the savage hunter too near
Our haunches not fast enough   our hunches inadequate
Our rare warmth once multiplied   now fading
in spite of the emerald and chartreuse patchwork
brilliant and billowing in the valley far below

These barren hills shorn by the sheep maintain
a long perspective of space   and time   the wind
blowing from the sea across this island land
There are many warrens here   but most
are emptied of wild lives

We scoot silently across the exposed field   ears alert
wary little hops of recognition towards each other
whiskered noses twitch with hesitancy
Angel clouds sail above   observing our tender follies
They seem to be relieved

The power of a narrative to change us all
Could this cold windswept hole
be an entrance to paradise?   Come with us
into the depth of the mountain   What marvels there!
Look closely   into the fur
camouflaged against dusty rock and weed
You can see our hearts pumping   our trembling
our fertile beauty

In the Greenhouse

I move among seamless fertility
measured by Visqueen light
translucent silence
and slow sexy beginnings
the smell of soil
moist   warm   funky

my hand reaches up
a smooth gesture dreamily weighted
to set strings as if on a lyre
daily the tendrils spiral round those strings
rise imperceptibly with steady botanical reserve
play music's lyric curve

Planting Spring Bulbs

the way this earth mounds up
sister
as new life surges
within you
I touch your belly
that rises
like the sun

In Between the Pansies and Hydrangea

this is what life should be like
it is what life is like
cool dark dirt
here, in between the pansies and hydrangea

though there's pain too
caution   local shadows
byzantine distances
who named this jungle anyway
where sleep is real   dreams too
there used to be eight trees no eight thousand
here, in between

why does it say not connected
when we are
what can I help you with
here, in between

where cold water startles
the brain electric
a harpist plays just around the corner
you're constantly in this
the birds chirp pink
decide to make a nest
between the pansies and hydrangea

with the power of your walk
eliminate the boundaries that prevent
natural time
here, in between

[…]

open your joints
sign agreements to share intellectual property
I invite you into the comfort of your space
we are belly breathers
lie down   here
feel the ground come up to meet you
in between the pansies and hydrangea

La Lune de Miel

(Honeymoon)

the hexagon of bee life
with precise points on which to rally
is so unlike the sway
of human curve
the slide or rise
geometry unbound
predictability unwound
with honey oozing over
every lip

– Acknowledgments –

Many thanks to the publications that brought these poems into the world, some in slightly different versions:

"California Buzz" first appeared in *Empty Space Places You* (Finishing Line Press, 2018)

"Cold Pizza for Breakfast" first appeared in *The Poeming Pigeon: Poems about Food* (The Poetry Box, 2015)

"Kiteboarder at Road's End" first appeared in *VoiceCatcher: a journal of women's voices & visions* (Summer, 2016)

∾

Thank you immensely to Shawn Aveningo Sanders and Robert Sanders at The Poetry Box for their willingness to publish *Bee Dance*. I am grateful for their warmth, enthusiasm, meticulous care, and easy cooperative ways during the entire process.

Special thanks to David Biespiel, Wendy Willis, Mary Szybist, and Andrea Hollander for reading some of these poems and for their insightful suggestions.

Also thanks to Carl Adamshick, John Morrison, Annie Lighthart, Paulann Petersen, Kim Stafford, and to the communities at the Attic Institute of Arts & Letters and the Mountain Writers Series for sharing the world of poetry.

Certainly my heartfelt gratitude goes to fellow writers Delia Tan Garigan, Phil Meehan, Anne Griffin Johnson, Brian Biggs, Betsy Porter, Celia Carlson, Margaret Chula, Tricia Knoll, Carolyn Martin, Pattie Palmer-Baker, and Shawn Aveningo Sanders for

[...]

their honest feedback about the poems in this collection, their encouragement, and just plain fun.

And deep appreciation to my sons, Alex and Max, and especially to my husband, Dan, for his unfailing companionship, his kindness and optimism, and for his trusted response to my work.

I am so fortunate and grateful, always, for the sustained support, good cheer, and inspiration of my dear extended family and friends.

– Praise for *Bee Dance* –

The energetic dance of bees at the hive focuses on describing a roadmap to abundance. Cathy Cain's poems in *Bee Dance* explore expanses of a world filled with animal and vegetative creatures. She describes the wordless comfort of holding a rock while acknowledging the spirit spaces between words. Her poetry expresses the impulse to reinvent ourselves outside of cyber noise and instead define ourselves within the boundaries of sentiencies around us. Her poems suggest trail guides through the perils of today's world that threaten lichens and suffocate us with plastics, moving us to landscapes of morning mist that say yes! and reveal honey in the communal hive.

— Tricia Knoll, author of *How I Learned to be White* and *Broadfork Farm*

Thrumming with a wise and generous curiosity, the poems in Cathy Cain's *Bee Dance* are bright signposts pointing a way forward through a difficult age. Whether about lichen, lava, or driving through a long tunnel, Cain's poems show us the pleasure of pattern and the possibility of imagination, of living with both grace and alarm. This book beautifully does poetry's steadfast work of naming and knowing the lives all around us. Here, the natural world meets the human over rich, porous boundaries: trees speak of long affection, stones quiet the mind, brushed hair sends off shooting stars. The poems in *Bee Dance* are blessings for the reader, as Cain's poem "Small Blessings" states so well: "One for each of us / so we know we're not alone."

— Annie Lighthart, author of *Lantern* and *Iron String*

– About the Author –

Poet and artist Cathy Cain is the author of *Empty Space Places You* (Finishing Line Press, 2018). Her honors include the Kay Snow Paulann Petersen Award for Poetry and the Edwin Markham Prize for Poetry. Her poetry has appeared in *Reed Magazine, VoiceCatcher, The Poeming Pigeon,* and *Verseweavers.*

Cain holds degrees in literature and visual art from Lewis & Clark College, MAT; Oregon State University, BFA; and University of Washington, BA, Phi Beta Kappa. She has studied at the Pacific Northwest College of Art, the Attic Institute of Arts and Letters, and with Portland's Mountain Writers Series.

The mother of two sons, Cain taught in the public schools for over thirty years. She lives with her husband near Portland, Oregon.

– About The Poetry Box® –

The Poetry Box was founded by Shawn Aveningo Sanders & Robert Sanders, who wholeheartedly believe that every day spent with the people you love, doing what you love, is a moment in life worth cherishing. Their boutique press celebrates the talents of their fellow artisans and writers through professional book design and publishing of individual collections, as well as their flagship literary journal, *The Poeming Pigeon*.

Feel free to visit the online bookstore (thePoetryBox.com), where you'll find more titles including:

The Way a Woman Knows by Carolyn Martin

Giving Ground by Lynn M. Knapp

Broadfork Farm by Tricia Knoll

Psyche's Scroll by Karla Linn Merrifield

November Quilt by Penelope Scambly Schott

Shrinking Bones by Judy K. Mosher

Epicurean Ecstasy by Cynthia Gallaher

The Poet's Curse by Michael Estabrook

Surreal Expulsion by D.R. James

The Unknowable Mystery of Other People by Sally Zakariya

Impossible Ledges by Dianne Avey

and more . . .